HOW TO LEAD A LIFE OF GODLINESS?

A HANDBOOK FOR LEADING A LIFE OF GODLINESS!

DAVID LIVINGSTON J

Contents

Foreword

This is what Billigraham says about Godliness

When a person accepts Jesus Christ as their Lord and Savior, they begin the sanctification process of becoming holy, or set apart. This means living a Godly life, which reflects the character of God. Although no one can be perfect like God, the Holy Spirit dwells in our hearts and helps us glorify God in our lives. Billy Graham said, "Make it your goal to become more like Christ by refusing to let sin have its way, and pursuing instead that which is pure and good in the sight of God."

Read 5 Bible verses about living a Godly life:

I appeal to you therefore, brothers, by the mercies of God, to present your bodies as a living sacrifice, holy and acceptable to God, which is your spiritual worship.Do not be conformed to this world, but be transformed by the renewal of your mind, that by testing you may discern what is the will of God, what is good and acceptable and perfect. (Romans 12:1-2)

Do your best to present yourself to God as one approved, a worker who does not need to be ashamed and who correctly handles the word of truth.Avoid godless chatter, because those who indulge in it will become more and more ungodly. (2 Timothy 2:15-16)

That all may honor the Son, just as they honor the Father. Whoever does not honor the Son does not honor the Father who sent him. (John 5:23)

As obedient children, do not conform to the evil desires you had when you lived in ignorance. But just as he who called you is holy, so be holy in all you do; for it is written: "Be holy, because I am holy." Since you call on a Father who judges each person's work impartially, live out your time as foreigners here in reverent fear. For you know that it was not with perishable things such as silver or gold that you were redeemed from the empty way of life handed down to you from your ancestors, but with the precious blood of Christ, a lamb without blemish or defect. (1 Peter 1:14-19)

Everything that I command you, you shall be careful to do. You shall not add to it or take from it. (Deuteronomy 12:32)

CHAPTER ONE

A Godly Generation!

"And did not he make one? Yet had he the residue of the spirit. And wherefore one? That he might seek a godly seed ..." (Malachi 2:15)

"So God created man in his own image, in the image of God he created him; male and female he created them." (Genesis 1:7)

The first Man Adam and his Wife!

In the beginning God created man in his own image, in the image of God created he him; He slammed him into the ground and blew his breath into him. Then life (spirit and soul) came into him. He became the soul of life. Adam was the first man to be created like that!

In the beginning there was only one man created by God. Not many. Do you know why? Because the pious offspring are to appear in this world through that one.

If God had made many people instead of one man, Adam, a pious people (dynasty) could not have appeared in this world. On the contrary, there might exist ungodliness and disrespect among human beings from the beginning. Every human being might have acted according to his own mental will and idea. Order could not have been found in society.

What is Godliness?

Godliness refers to man's relationship with the God who created him (the Creator). A pious person will have the following characteristics:

1. He believes that God exists. That is, he believes that he did not naturally appear in this world and that there is a God who made him.

2. He wants to have a daily relationship with God. He seeks His fellowship (presence) day and night; He longs God to be with him all the time.

3. He wants to do things that are pleasing to God. He will try to give God his due respect; He will also worship and serve the living God all the days of his life.

One day a thief broke into a houste at night to steal. The owner of the house is devout. He trusted in God and slept peacefully. The thief entered the house and went straight into the room housing the bureau. He opened the bureau and stolen a bundle of money and jewelry.

As he was about to take everything he had finished, he suddenly had a stomach ache that came as usual. He could not bear that stomach ache. He didn't know what to do and how to handle the situation.

As he was throbbing with stomach ache he saw a picture of Jesus Christ hanging on the wall. A thought arose in his mind: "Why not call on Jesus Christ once?" He immediately confessed his sins to Jesus: "Jesus, forgive me. And relieve me from this stomach ache; I will not steal anymore."

Immediately the abdominal pain left him. He left everything he had stolen and went back. He found happiness and peace. What a change he had in his life!

Yes, there was a kind of devotion found within that thief. So he got forgiveness of sins and physical happiness! May we take a moment to reflect on how our devotion is today?

CHAPTER TWO

The first Godly Family on Earth!

And the Lord God commanded the man, 'You are free to eat from any tree in the garden; but you must not eat from the tree of the knowledge of good and evil, for when you eat from it you will certainly die."

The Lord God said, "It is not good for the man to be alone. I will make a helper suitable for him." (Genesis 2:16-18)

Tree of Life and the tree of Knowledge of Good and Evil

God made Adam and made him live in the garden of Eden. In the garden God planted all kinds of fruit trees Adam needed. In the middle of the garden, God caused two trees to grow. One of them was tree of Life; and the other one is the tree of Knowledge of good and evil.

God put Adam the incharge of such a fruit-bearing garden and gave him the task of cultivating and preserving it. He also gave him the power to rule over all the birds, animals, reptiles, and sea creatures that he had created.

After that, God gave Adam only one commandment, that he should obey. The command is that he may pluck all the fruit of the garden and eat. But he shall not eat fruit from the tree of Knowledge of good and evil. He also said that he would die on the day he ate it.

God saw that it was not good for Adam, the man he had made, to be alone in that garden. God caused Adam to have a deep sleep and took one of the bones from his ribs and made a woman out of it. Adam named her Eve. She was the mother of all living human beings.

Adam and Eve began their home life happily in the garden of Eden. They enjoyed having fellowship with God every morning. They lead a godly life in the garden of Eden keeping the commandment given by the Lord.

Fall of Adam and Eve:

One day the enemy, Satan, entered the garden of Eden in the form of a serpent and started a conversation with Eve. In response, Eve talked to him when she was alone in a part of the garden. At the end of the conversation Eve had with Satan, she was seduced with his lying words.

The woman who was deceived by Satan plucked the fruit of the tree of Knowledge of good and evil which God forbade to eat and gave it to her husband. Adam bought it from Eve and ate it, disobeying God's command. In this way, sin entered into that first family of Adam and Eve.

So the Lord God said to the serpent, "Because you have done this,

"Cursed are you above all livestock and all wild animals! You will crawl on your belly and you will eat dust all the days of your life.

And I will put enmity between you and the woman, and between your offspring[a] and hers; he will crush your head, and you will strike his heel." (Genesis 3:14-15)

Satan sought to thwart God's plan by turning the godly family (Adam - Eve) into sin. But our God is infinitely wise. He had a plan to remove the ungodliness that came through sin. That is the "**seed of the woman.**"

Seed of the Woman:

The plan is for God, who created man, to be born in the womb of a virgin, to accept the sin of man's transgression, and to give man forgiveness, holiness, and true godliness.

After sinning, God expelled Adam and his wife, Eve, from the garden. Because the man who accepted death by eating the fruit of the knowledge of good and evil should not pluck the fruit of the tree of Life in the middle of the garden and live forever as the doer of evil.

Although expelled from the garden, they were not completely excluded from God's presence (direct control). Yet because of sin they could not have a relationship with God as before. They have gone a little farther from God. Sin caused division between God and man.

Cain and Abel:

Adam made love to his wife Eve, and she became pregnant and gave birth to Cain.

She said, "With the help of the Lord I have brought forth a man."

Later she gave birth to his brother Abel.Now Abel kept flocks, and Cain worked the soil. (Genesis 4:1-2)

Adam, who lost his blessing of having eternal relationship with God as a result of sin, began to continue his family life on earth. Sons were born to him. Their names were **Cain** and **Abel**. Cain was the eldest; Abel was the youngest. As they grew old, ungodliness was found within Cain; But Abel was found to be godly.

One day they both came to give thanks to God. God recognized Abel and his offering. But, God did not recognize Cain, because his heart was not pure before God.

Cain was irritated when he saw that God did not approve of him and his offering. He hated his brother Abel. Then one day when they were alone, Cain rose up against Abel and killed him.

CHAPTER THREE

Knowledge of Good and Evil!

And the Lord God said, "The man has now become like one of us, knowing good and evil. He must not be allowed to reach out his hand and take also from the tree of life and eat, and live forever." (Genesis 3:22)

Adam and Eve sent out of Garden of Eden

So the Lord God banished him from the Garden of Eden to work the ground from which he had been taken.

After he drove the man out, he placed on the east side of the Garden of Eden cherubim and a flaming sword flashing back and forth to guard the way to the tree of life. (Genesis 3:23, 24)

God put two things before man: one is life and the other one is death. He placed both of them before him in two different trees as fruit. He also gave Adam the power to think and act on his own. But through his disobedience what man chosen was not life but death.

Adam could have survived death and lived forever if he had plucked the fruit of the tree of life. Instead, Adam and Eve ate the fruit of tree of Knowledge of good and evil and accepted death.

Spirit, Soul and Body:

When Adam was created by God, three realms were found within him: the spirit, soul and the body. Both the spirit and the soul are hidden within the body and hence we call them (both soul and spirit) the inner man. The outer body is made up of flesh and blood.

The bodily outer man looks like a tent containing the spirit and the soul. As soon as the first man (Adam) accepted death by disobedience, immediate death occurred in the inner man. Days passed before the physical death occurred. This can be seen in Genesis 5: 4-5:

After Seth was born, Adam lived 800 years and had other sons and daughters. Altogether, Adam lived a total of 930 years, and then he died.

Knowledge of Good and Evil:

Man, who was made to know only good, knew what evil was because he plucked and ate the fruit of the tree of Knowledge of good and evil. Having inherited the knowledge of both good and evil, adam and his generation were liable to cling to evil rather than good.

This is what God expected of Adam and his descendants after Adam sinned: **as a sinful man, who knows good and evil, one should hate evil and embrace good.** But man began to know evil more than good. We see this in the life of Cain, the son of Adam. In Genesis 4: 6-8 we read:

Then the Lord said to Cain, "Why are you angry? Why is your face downcast?

If you do what is right, will you not be accepted? But if you do not do what is right, sin is crouching at your door; it desires to have you, but you must rule over it."

Now Cain said to his brother Abel, "Let's go out to the field." While they were in the field, Cain attacked his brother Abel and killed him.

After killing Abel, Cain answered God when he was asked, "Where is Abel?": "I did not know where he was; Am I guarding him?" (Genesis 4: 9). Cain, who was supposed to protect his brother and do good to him, rose up against him and did evil to him. So he received a curse from God.

Cain and his Descendants!

Do not be like Cain, who belonged to the evil one and murdered his brother. And why did he murder him? Because his own actions were evil and his brother's were righteous. (I John 3:12)

Cain - the Brother of Abel

Woe to them! They have taken the way of Cain; they have rushed for profit into Balaam's error; they have been destroyed in Korah's rebellion. (Jude 11)

Scripture says of Cain:

1. He belonged to the evil one (Satan). Though Cain was given by God as the eldest son of Adam and Eve, he gave place to the evil one - Satan and became his child.

2. He was seen walking in a wicked way. When he saw that God did not approve of himself and his offering , he was irritated and his countenance fell.

3. His deeds were evil. He chose to do evil (harm) rather than good to his brother Abel. So he killed his brother Abel.

The first generation of Adam saw the grave sin of "murder." Man began to commit sin upon sin. As a result, man completely lost his unity (relationship) with God. Cain after murding Abel, his brother, went out of the presence (fellowship) of God and became the father of an ungodly generation. The pious and righteous Abel disappeared from this world.

Lamech - a Descendant of Cain!

Cain made love to his wife, and she became pregnant and gave birth to Enoch. Cain was then building a city, and he named it after his son Enoch.

To Enoch was born Irad, and Irad was the father of Mehujael, and Mehujael was the father of Methushael, and Methushael was the father of Lamech.

Lamech married two women, one named Adah and the other Zillah. (Genesis 4:17-19)

Lamech said to his wives, "Adah and Zillah, listen to me; wives of Lamech, hear my words. I have killed a man for wounding me, a young man for injuring me." (Genesis 4:23)

Lamech was the fifth generation of the descendants of Cain, who killed Abel. This Lamech followed in the footsteps of his ancestor Cain and killed a young man who had wounded himself. He made it known to his wives.

Lamech not only walked in the way of Cain but also broke the oath of oneness which is the ordinance of God. Lamech was the first to marry two women and lead a family life. The descendants of Cain left a false mark on future generations.

As the days go by it has become a culture to live with more than one wife. To this day there are many among us who walk in the ways of Cain and Lamech.

Murder, adultery and fornication are considered as the works of the flesh. Galatians chapter 5 verses 19 to 21 list out the sins that are committed as the works of the flesh.

The acts of the flesh are obvious: sexual immorality, impurity and debauchery; idolatry and witchcraft; hatred, discord, jealousy, fits of rage, selfish ambition, dissensions, factions and envy; drunkenness, orgies, and the like. I warn you, as I did before, that those who live like this will not inherit the kingdom of God.

If any of these works of the flesh are found in us, we cannot enter into the **Kingdom of Heaven**, which is called the **Kingdom of God**. Only when we repent of such sins and become new creatures do we become worthy of heavenly life.

Decesdants of Cain Destroyed!

Cain did not repent of the sin of killing his brother Abel. Instead he wanted to build a city for himself and his descendants and to live in it safely. Scripture therefore does not indicate how many years he lived on the face of the earth.

Perhaps Cain's soul was the first soul to go to hell, the place of death and torment. Not only that, but Cain's descendants were wiped out centuries later by the great Flood on earth. So let us not live like Cain and Lamech, but let us fear the Lord and walk in his commandments.

The period in which Cain and his descendants lived is called the **age of conscience**. That is, God guided people by giving them the knowledge of what is good and what is bad in their conscience. Spoke to them by conscience and sometimes spoke to them directly.

But the ungodly men who lived in those days did not obey it. Instead they lived adventurously. They did what their minds and flesh wanted and sinned against God. So they were judged by God and perished.